This journal belongs to

....

Date

....

Ellie Claire
Hachette Book Group
1290 Avenue of the Americas, New York, NY 10104
ellieclaire.com

First edition: September 2019

Ellie Claire is a division of Hachette Book Group, Inc. The Ellie Claire name and logo are trademarks of Hachette Book Group, Inc. The publisher is not responsible for websites (or their content) that are not owned by the publisher.

Compiled by Jill Olson.
Print book interior design by Bart Dawson.

ISBN: 9781546014492 (Leatherluxe®)

Printed in the China
RRD-S
10 9 8 7 6 5 4 3 2 1

CONTENTS

INTRODUCTION

*C*ountless numbers of people are walking around wounded in their souls from past hurts, and they either don't know they can be healed or simply don't know what to do or how to begin. In the book and workbook *Healing the Soul of a Woman*, I have shared what I have learned on my journey about overcoming those wounds. And although your journey won't be exactly like mine, I hope my story can be an inspiration and a guiding light as you step out onto your path of progress toward wholeness.

As you work through the questions and activities in this journal, I pray you will discover the beautiful gift of healing God wants to give you, His beloved. Contemplate areas where you need healing and ask God to activate healing in your life.

But also remember that healing takes time. It is sometimes painful because we have to let old wounds be opened up in order to get the infection that is festering and poisoning our souls out of them. Women who have need of healing for their soul only have two choices. The first is to continue limping along in life, just trying to get through each day, and the second is to say, "I've had enough misery, unhappiness, pretense, guilt, and shame, and I'm ready to do whatever it takes to be made whole!"

I hope this journal becomes the safe place for you to do the work of overcoming, of becoming healed and whole!

Joyce Meyer

Chapter 1

THE HISTORY OF WOMEN

*W*omen are God's idea.... The battle for the freedom and restoration of women is ongoing, but I am glad I know that healing can occur through faith in God, and I am glad that our ministry is part of helping to bring this freedom to women worldwide.... Thankfully, our history does not have to be our destiny.

The LORD God caused a deep sleep to fall on Adam, and he slept;

and He took one of his ribs, and closed up the flesh in its place.

Then the rib which the LORD God had taken from man He made

into a woman, and He brought her to the man. And Adam said:

"This is now bone of my bones and flesh of my flesh."

GENESIS 2:21–23 NKJV

*H*ow does the following quote connect to the theme of this chapter? How can it influence your personal journey of soul healing?

Make the most of yourself, by fanning the tiny sparks of possibility into flames of achievement. —GOLDA MEIR

....

....

....

....

....

....

....

....

....

....

....

....

....

....

....

....

....

....

....

....

To help you get in touch with your inner self, use the lines below to reflect on your attitude toward yourself. Is it healthy? What specifically would you like to change? Set a goal for change, then write a prayer of praise to God for your coming restoration and redirected battles.

*D*escribe the battles you are fighting. Write a prayer that you can repeat as often as needed asking God to fight these battles for you. If needed, include a request for God to show you His original plan for the respectful, peaceful coexistence of men and women,

....

....

....

....

....

....

....

....

....

....

....

....

....

....

....

....

....

....

....

....

"Believe me when I say that when God fights on your side,

you always win!"

Let this same attitude and purpose and [humble] mind be in you which was in Christ Jesus: [Let Him be your example in humility.] —PHILIPPIANS 2:5

*W*hat does this Bible verse mean to you? Where do you see opportunities in your life to adjust your attitude to become more humble, like Christ?

....

....

....

....

....

....

....

....

....

....

....

....

....

....

....

....

....

....

....

....

....

....

*S*pend time in prayer, asking God to reveal any people, situations, or circumstances in your life that consistently derail your attitude. Record them below, and praise God for His ability to heal and restore you.

....

....

....

....

....

....

....

....

....

....

....

....

....

....

....

....

....

....

....

....

"I didn't have a good start in life,
but I am determined to have a good finish!"

Chapter 2

LIVING THE BEST LIFE AVAILABLE

*I*n the very early days of Christianity, it was often called "the Way." God's plan includes a way to live that will lead us to everything good He offers.... Once you are born again (repent of sin and receive Jesus as Savior), you no longer need to be led by rules and regulations, expecting to get some reward from God if you keep them all, but you can be led and prompted by the Holy Spirit, who will guide you into the full plan of God for your life. It truly is a whole new way of living.

The thief comes only in order to steal and kill and destroy.
I came that they may have and enjoy life,
and have it in abundance (to the full, till it overflows).

JOHN 10:10

*H*ow does the following quote connect to the theme of this chapter? How can it influence your personal journey of soul healing?

In Him was Life, and the Life was the Light of men. —John 1:4

....

....

....

....

....

....

....

....

....

....

....

....

....

....

....

....

....

....

....

....

....

*I*s your relationship with God due for an upgrade? Are there areas in your life where you are now working with God and His plan for your life that you weren't last year, or five years ago? Explain. Describe what you would like your relationship with Him to be like.

....

....

....

....

....

....

....

....

....

....

....

....

....

....

....

....

....

....

....

....

....

....

*D*o you want all God has for you? Write a prayer of commitment to learning how to enjoy the best life God has available to you through Jesus Christ.

....
....
....
....
....
....
....
....
....
....
....
....
....
....
....
....
....
....
....
....
....
....
....
....
....
....
....

"Just as you have to learn how to work the new upgrade
you get, we have to learn how to work with God
and His plan for our lives."

*We are God's [own] handiwork (His workmanship), recreated in Christ Jesus,
[born anew] that we may do those good works which God predestined
(planned beforehand) for us [taking paths which He prepared ahead of time],
that we should walk in them [living the good life which He prearranged
and made ready for us to live].* —EPHESIANS 2:10

*W*hat does this Bible verse mean to you? What is the difference between
something made by a worker on an assembly line and something that displays
a creator's workmanship?

....

....

....

....

....

....

....

....

....

....

....

....

....

....

....

....

*C*ommit to studying God's Word daily. Use the lines below to write a plan for a daily reading/meditation time, and to keep track of the insight you are gaining.

....

....

....

....

....

....

....

....

....

....

....

....

....

....

....

....

....

....

....

....

....

....

....

....

"As I studied God's Word and applied what I was learning,
amazing changes began to happen in me—in my soul."

Chapter 3

GOD WANTS THE WOUNDED

*G*od wants soldiers in His army who have allowed Him to heal their wounded souls.... God actually uses our wounds to give us wisdom and to equip us to bring light into the darkness of other wounded souls.

God selected (deliberately chose) what in the world is foolish to put the wise to shame, and what the world calls weak to put the strong to shame. And God also selected (deliberately chose) what in the world is lowborn and insignificant and branded and treated with contempt, even the things that are nothing, that He might depose and bring to nothing the things that are.

1 CORINTHIANS 1:27–28

*H*ow does the following quote connect to the theme of this chapter? How can it influence your personal journey of soul healing?

The unwounded life bears no resemblance to the Rabbi. —Brennan Manning

....

....

....

....

....

....

....

....

....

....

....

....

....

....

....

....

....

....

....

....

....

....

....

....

....

....

....

....

*C*an you identify the wisdom you have gained from each of your wounds? If not, take a few minutes to ask God about it, then record below what He impresses on your heart.

....
....
....
....
....
....
....
....
....
....
....
....
....
....
....
....
....
....
....
....
....
....
....

*D*o you believe that through your wounds, God will turn you into a valuable tool that can be used to help those who are seeking help? Write a prayer of faith, confessing your belief that God will use you as a new, fresh threshing instrument (see Isaiah 41:15–17).

....

....

....

....

....

....

....

....

....

....

....

....

....

....

....

....

....

....

....

*"Multitudes of people have mountains looming in front of them
that they feel they can never overcome, but you can use
your experience to help them."*

For [simply] consider your own call, brethren; not many [of you were considered to be] wise according to human estimates and standards, not many influential and powerful, not many of high and noble birth. —1 CORINTHIANS 1:26

*W*hat does this Bible verse mean to you? In light of what you've been through in your life, what do you believe God is or might be calling you to do?

....

....

....

....

....

....

....

....

....

....

....

....

....

....

....

....

....

....

....

....

*U*se the lines below to officially offer each wound in your life to God for His use.

....
....
....
....
....
....
....
....
....
....
....
....
....
....
....
....
....
....
....
....
....
....

"I vividly recall saying to God, 'I am a broken mess,
but I'm Yours if You can use me,' and He did.
Anything we give to God will never be wasted."

"We are prone to despising the painful things we have gone through in life, but God can use them to help others if we will let Him. I don't for one second believe that God arranged for my abuse so He could give me some experience, but I do believe that He has used my experience to help other people, and He will do the same thing with your experience in life."

Chapter 4

WHAT IS A HEALTHY SOUL?

*O*ur thoughts have an amazing effect on us. The apostle Paul teaches that God has a wonderful plan for our lives, but in order to see it happen, we must have our minds completely renewed.

Do not be conformed to this world,
but be transformed by the renewal of your mind,
that by testing you may discern what is the will of God,
what is good and acceptable and perfect.

ROMANS 12:2 ESV

*H*ow does the following quote connect to the theme of this chapter? How can it influence your personal journey of soul healing?

Truly my soul finds rest in God; my salvation comes from him. —PSALM 62:1 NIV

....

....

....

....

....

....

....

....

....

....

....

....

....

....

....

....

....

....

....

....

....

....

....

....

....

*W*hat would a day of *resting in God* look like for you? Start with your thoughts in the morning before your feet hit the floor, and end when you are lying in bed at night.

....

....

....

....

....

....

....

....

....

....

....

....

....

....

....

....

....

....

....

....

....

....

*W*hat foundation are you building your life on? Write a prayer that you can repeat as often as needed, expressing your belief in God above your feelings, your desires, or your thoughts.

....
....
....
....
....
....
....
....
....
....
....
....
....
....
....
....
....
....

"He does and always will take care of us because He loves us
unconditionally.... His promises are greater and more worthy
of our trust than anything else. All else is shifting sand,
but His Word is lasting and endures forever."

Take My yoke upon you and learn of Me, for I am gentle (meek) and humble (lowly) in heart, and you will find rest (relief and ease and refreshment and recreation and blessed quiet) for your souls. —MATTHEW 11:29

*W*hat does this Bible verse mean to you? What is causing the most disquiet in your soul? Personalize this verse as a prayer, expressing your trust in Jesus's gentle and humble ways.

....

....

....

....

....

....

....

....

....

....

....

....

....

....

....

....

....

....

....

....

....

A big part of freedom is learning to control our response to what takes place around us. In the lines below, keep track of your little-by-little victories.

....

....

....

....

....

....

....

....

....

....

....

....

....

....

....

....

....

....

....

....

"It is important to remember that God has promised that He will complete the good work He has begun in us (Philippians 1:6). Our part is to keep pressing toward the goal and to never give up. Eventually, little by little, our soul will find its rest in God."

Chapter 5

HELP ME!
I DON'T UNDERSTAND MYSELF

*L*earning to understand the root of our behaviors is vital to changing them. Studying God's Word helps us gain insight.... Don't be afraid to walk in the light with God and let Him reveal truth to You.

You have delivered my life from death, yes,
and my feet from falling, that I may walk before God
in the light of life and of the living.

PSALM 56:13

How does the following quote connect to the theme of this chapter? How can it influence your personal journey of soul healing?

The most difficult thing in life is to know yourself. —THALES

....

....

....

....

....

....

....

....

....

....

....

....

....

....

....

....

....

....

....

....

$\mathcal{B}$efore we can be free from the things that steal our peace and joy, it is crucial to slow down and face the truth. Write a prayer asking for help slowing down, and for the Holy Spirit to give you discernment into the root of your problems.

....

....

....

....

....

....

....

....

....

....

....

....

....

....

....

....

....

....

....

....

....

....

....

*T*hink about the last time you had a bad or unusual reaction to a person or situation. Ask God to help you understand why you behaved as you did, and record the specific insight He gives you below.

....
....
....
....
....
....
....
....
....
....
....
....
....
....
....
....
....
....
....

"Learning to understand the root of our behaviors
is vital to changing them.
Studying God's Word helps us gain insight."

So let's not get tired of doing what is good. At just the right time we will reap a harvest of blessing if we don't give up. —GALATIANS 6:9 NLT

*W*hat does this Bible verse mean to you? How would you describe the "harvest of blessing" you are looking for? Rewrite the second sentence of this verse with your name in it.

....

....

....

....

....

....

....

....

....

....

....

....

....

....

....

....

....

....

....

....

se this space to record ongoing behavior problems, along with your underlying motivation, as God reveals it to you. Praise Him for the restoration He will bring with each revelation.

....
....
....
....
....
....
....
....
....
....
....
....
....
....
....
....
....
....
....
....
....
....
....

"Be a lifetime learner, especially about yourself.
There is an amazing person inside of you waiting to come out!"

Chapter 6

YOU ARE GOD'S BELOVED

*R*eceiving love seems to be especially difficult for those of us who have been deeply wounded in our lives, but once we begin to receive God's love, we find that love is the healing balm our souls need...it also gives us confidence and courage.

And we know (understand, recognize, are conscious of,
by observation and by experience) and believe (adhere to and
put faith in and rely on) the love God cherishes for us. God is love,
and he who dwells and continues in love dwells and continues in God,
and God dwells and continues in him.

1 JOHN 4:16

*H*ow does the following quote connect to the theme of this chapter? How can it influence your personal journey of soul healing?

> *Beloved, now we are children of God; and it has not yet been revealed*
> *what we shall be, but we know that when He is revealed, we shall be like Him,*
> *for we shall see Him as He is.* —1 JOHN 3:2 NKJV

....

....

....

....

....

....

....

....

....

....

....

....

....

....

....

....

....

....

....

....

....

*W*hat does it mean to be the beloved of God? Write "I am God's beloved." Now write it with your name inserted in the sentence. Say it out loud. Do you realize what you just testified to is something God desires you to believe in the deepest part of you?

*I*f you could ask God to take any fear from your life, what would it be? Write a prayer, trusting that fear to Jesus, stating your belief that His perfect love will cast out your fear.

....

....

....

....

....

....

....

....

....

....

....

....

....

....

....

....

....

....

....

....

....

....

....

....

....

....

"When we have a deep revelation of God's love for us,
it enables us to stand firm through the trials of life."

*May Christ through your faith [actually] dwell (settle down, abide,
make His permanent home) in your hearts! May you be rooted deep in love
and founded securely on love. —*EPHESIANS 3:17

*W*hat does this Bible verse mean to you? How does someone become rooted
deeply in love? Have you made it a habit to watch for God's love during your day,
not taking any blessing as coincidence? What blessings have you seen lately?

....

....

....

....

....

....

....

....

....

....

....

....

....

....

....

....

....

....

*R*ecord your favorite verses that tell of His love, inserting your name into the verse. (Suggestions: Romans 8:35; Ephesians 2:4–5; and 1 Thessalonians 1:4)

Example:
Who shall ever separate Joyce from Christ's love?

....

....

....

....

....

....

....

....

....

....

....

....

....

....

....

....

....

....

....

....

....

*"As I diligently studied and meditated on what the Bible teaches
about how much God loves us and learned to watch for His love
in my life, I finally began to feel loved."*

"God says in His Word that He has loved your life back from the pit of corruption and nothingness (Isaiah 38:17).

Jesus was sent to heal the brokenhearted, to bind up their wounds and heal their bruises (Isaiah 61:1).

Let His love begin to do the work in your wounded soul that it is intended to do!"

Chapter 7

Hurting People Hurt People

*T*he devil's plan is for us to continue living with the pain of our past and to wound others, from generation to generation, preventing anyone from enjoying what Jesus died to give them. But Jesus gave us instructions about how we can defeat the devil and not have our history become our destiny.

Love your enemies and be kind and do good [doing favors
so that someone derives benefit from them] and lend, expecting
and hoping for nothing in return but considering nothing as lost and
despairing of no one; and then your recompense (your reward)
will be great (rich, strong, intense, and abundant),
and you will be sons of the Most High, for He is kind and charitable
and good to the ungrateful and the selfish and wicked.

Luke 6:35

*H*ow does the following quote connect to the theme of this chapter? How can it influence your personal journey of soul healing?

Beloved, never avenge yourselves, but leave the way open
for [God's] wrath; for it is written, Vengeance is Mine,
I will repay (requite), says the Lord. —ROMANS 12:19

....
....
....
....
....
....
....
....
....
....
....
....
....
....
....
....
....
....
....
....
....

*A*re there things in your past that you need to give over to God for avenging? Write a specific prayer of release, trusting in God to repay those wrongs done to you.

....

....

....

....

....

....

....

....

....

....

....

....

....

....

....

....

....

....

....

....

....

....

$\mathcal{S}$trongholds lose power over us when we bring them to the light. Write a prayer to repeat often, asking God to reveal any area(s) of hidden unforgiveness in your life.

....

....

....

....

....

....

....

....

....

....

....

....

....

....

....

....

....

....

....

....

....

"I believe that forgiving the people who hurt us is the single most powerful thing we will ever do. It releases us from emotional torment and frees us to get on with life."

Instead of your [former] shame you shall have a twofold recompense;
instead of dishonor and reproach [your people] shall rejoice in their portion.
Therefore in their land they shall possess double [what they had forfeited];
everlasting joy shall be theirs. —ISAIAH 61:7

*W*hat does this Bible verse mean to you? What shame are you willing to forfeit for God's promised twofold recompense?

....

....

....

....

....

....

....

....

....

....

....

....

....

....

....

....

....

....

*M*ake that powerful step. Write a statement of forgiveness for each area of resentment that God has revealed to you.

....

....

....

....

....

....

....

....

....

....

....

....

....

....

....

....

....

....

*"Everything He asks us to do is for our benefit
and the benefit of those we are doing life with."*

Chapter 8

Unload the Guilt and Shame

*B*roken and wounded people absolutely cannot recover until they unload the guilt and shame that they carry. We have all made mistakes in life, and we have all done things that we are ashamed of, but being ashamed of something we have done, or even something that was done to us, is totally different than internalizing the shame and becoming ashamed of ourselves.

He was wounded for our transgressions, He was bruised
for our guilt and iniquities; the chastisement [needful to obtain]
peace and well-being for us was upon Him, and with the stripes
[that wounded] Him we are healed and made whole.

Isaiah 53:5

*H*ow does the following quote connect to the theme of this chapter? How can it influence your personal journey of soul healing?

Fear not, for you shall not be ashamed; neither be confounded and depressed, for you shall not be put to shame. For you shall forget the shame of your youth, and you shall not [seriously] remember the reproach of your widowhood any more. —ISAIAH 54:4

....

....

....

....

....

....

....

....

....

....

....

....

....

....

....

....

....

....

....

....

....

*T*ake a stand against any shame and guilt that loads you down by asking forgiveness for any unconfessed offenses. Then get on with your life—don't continue to feel guilty! Write a statement of belief in God's Word over your feelings that you can confess every time shame and guilt try to creep back.

....

....

....

....

....

....

....

....

....

....

....

....

....

....

....

....

....

....

....

....

....

....

The Bible says that we are to put on righteousness (Ephesians 6:14). To "put it on" means to firmly believe it and learn to walk with the dignity God offers you as His precious, valuable child. Do you see yourself as having dignity? Write a letter to God, thanking Him for the dignity that is already yours as His daughter, because of Jesus.

....
....
....
....
....
....
....
....
....
....
....
....
....
....
....
....
....
....
....
....

"If you still suffer with feelings of guilt and shame,
you need more revelation about who you are in Christ."

I heard a loud voice in heaven, saying, "Now the salvation and the power and the kingdom of our God and the authority of his Christ have come, for the accuser of our brothers has been thrown down, who accuses them day and night before our God. —REVELATION 12:10 ESV

*W*hat does this Bible verse mean to you? Every thought you have is not necessarily the truth, no matter how convincing it feels. Ask God to reveal the accusations that you have believed, and expose them on paper here.

....

....

....

....

....

....

....

....

....

....

....

....

....

....

....

....

....

....

....

....

....

....

....

*W*e overcome Satan by the blood of Christ, the Word of God, and our testimony (Revelation 12:11). Part of your testimony is that you are a redeemed, powerful child of God, who is filled with possibility and potential. Make a list of promises from Scripture regarding your identity to confess them daily.

....

....

....

....

....

....

....

....

....

....

....

....

....

....

....

....

....

....

....

....

....

"After over forty years of studying and teaching God's Word, I still confess each day that I am the righteousness of God in Christ."

Chapter 9

FINDING YOUR TRUE SELF

*W*hen we receive Jesus as our Savior, according to Scripture, we are born again, or born anew. It is a point in our lives where we are invited to let go of anything old and fully become the amazing person that God originally intended us to be before our experience with the world and sin wounded us.

Strip yourselves of your former nature [put off and discard your old unrenewed self] which characterized your previous manner of life and becomes corrupt through lusts and desires that spring from delusion; and be constantly renewed in the spirit of your mind [having a fresh mental and spiritual attitude], and put on the new nature (the regenerate self) created in God's image, [Godlike] in true righteousness and holiness.

EPHESIANS 4:22-24

*H*ow does the following quote connect to the theme of this chapter? How can it influence *your personal journey of soul healing?*

Therefore, if anyone is in Christ, he is a new creation. The old has passed away; behold, the new has come. —2 CORINTHIANS 5:17 ESV

....

....

....

....

....

....

....

....

....

....

....

....

....

....

....

....

....

....

....

....

*O*n a scale of one to ten, how comfortable are you being you? How does that number change, depending on who you are with? Explain. What is standing in the way of you being you?

....

....

....

....

....

....

....

....

....

....

....

....

....

....

....

....

....

....

....

....

....

*H*ave you ever taken the time to search your heart to discover what you love? If you haven't, first ask God to give you clarity on your own heart, then write some of the things that come to mind. Write a prayer, asking God for the courage and direction in Christ to start doing what He created you to do.

"*You do have a real life, a true self,*
but it can only be found in Christ."

You are a chosen race, a royal priesthood, a dedicated nation,
[God's] own purchased, special people, that you may set forth
the wonderful deeds and display the virtues and perfections of Him
Who called you out of darkness into His marvelous light. —1 PETER 2:9

*W*hat does this Bible verse mean to you? How might your strengths display the virtues and perfections of God?

....

....

....

....

....

....

....

....

....

....

....

....

....

....

....

....

....

....

....

....

....

....

*T*hink about some of the labels you have felt from others or yourself. Now record them below, followed by the truth of God's Word. Speak those verses aloud daily, or whenever you feel labeled.

Example:
LABEL: She never finishes anything.
GOD'S TRUTH: Psalm 138:8—You will accomplish what concerns me;
You lovingkindness, O Lord, is everlasting.

"Our true self is one who is the beloved of God.
Every other identity is a false one."

"The shame had to be dealt with,
and it was through taking God at His word,
instead of continuing to be controlled
by my thoughts and emotions,
that I was finally set free."

Chapter 10

NO PARKING AT ANY TIME

*A*s God's daughter, you are a new creature. All of the old things have passed away and all things are made new (2 Corinthians 5:17). Accept that truth found in God's Word as your new normal and refuse to park at the point of your pain.

I do not consider, brethren, that I have captured and
made it my own [yet]; but one thing I do [it is my one aspiration]:
forgetting what lies behind and straining forward
to what lies ahead, I press on toward the goal to win
the [supreme and heavenly] prize to which
God in Christ Jesus is calling us upward.

PHILIPPIANS 3:13–14

How does the following quote connect to the theme of this chapter? How can it influence your personal journey of soul healing?

The Lord said to Moses, Why do you cry to Me?
Tell the people of Israel to go forward! —EXODUS 14:15

....

....

....

....

....

....

....

....

....

....

....

....

....

....

....

....

....

....

....

....

....

....

....

....

*H*ave you parked your dreams at the place of your pain? What is the point of your pain? What would moving forward look like for you?

....

....

....

....

....

....

....

....

....

....

....

....

....

....

....

....

....

....

....

....

....

....

....

....

*B*eing successful is a continual state of being. What daily habits can you set up in your life to reach that continual state of being?

"God created us to be people who are always moving forward.
Being successful in anything isn't a one-time achievement."

*For I know the thoughts and plans that I have for you, says the Lord,
thoughts and plans for welfare and peace and not for evil,
to give you hope in your final outcome.* —JEREMIAH 29:11

*W*hat does this Bible verse mean to you? Do you wake up every morning knowing that God has a future for you in that day, one that is adding to a bigger future picture? What could He be using from today to prepare you for your future?

....

....

....

....

....

....

....

....

....

....

....

....

....

....

....

....

....

....

....

*P*ray about how God would have you move forward, away from your place of pain, then list what you feel He is telling you below.

....

....

....

....

....

....

....

....

....

....

....

....

....

....

....

....

....

....

*"Jesus is our Healer, but there will be things that He asks us
to do on our journey, and if we don't do them, then
we won't experience the healing He is making available."*

Chapter 11

YOU ARE NOT DAMAGED GOODS

*G*od offers us a new beginning, and that means we must put the past behind us and not look back. Let go of all blame, shame, and guilt from the past, and let God show Himself strong in your life.

My grace (My favor and loving-kindness and mercy) is enough
for you [sufficient against any danger and enables you
to bear the trouble manfully]; for My strength and power
are made perfect (fulfilled and completed) and
show themselves most effective in [your] weakness.

2 CORINTHIANS 12:9

*H*ow does the following quote connect to the theme of this chapter? How can it influence your personal journey of soul healing?

> *In Him you have been made complete, and He is the head*
> *over all rule and authority.* —COLOSSIANS 2:10 NASB

....

....

....

....

....

....

....

....

....

....

....

....

....

....

....

....

....

....

....

....

....

*H*ave you settled for less than God's best? How? What is the beauty of our weaknesses (see 2 Corinthians 12:9)?

....

....

....

....

....

....

....

....

....

....

....

....

....

....

....

....

....

....

....

....

....

....

....

....

....

*T*hink of the weaknesses you perceive in yourself, then write a prayer thanking God that You are complete in Christ, that any weaknesses you have will showcase His glory.

....
....
....
....
....
....
....
....
....
....
....
....
....
....
....
....
....
....
....

"Jesus paid a high price for our healing and restoration when He died on the cross, so let's start receiving the benefits He purchased for us with His sacrifice."

The fire had no power upon their bodies, nor was the hair of their head singed; neither were their garments scorched or changed in color or condition, nor had even the smell of smoke clung to them. —DANIEL 3:27

What does this Bible verse mean to you? Tell about a difficulty in your life, and write out a prayer of trust that God will totally deliver you from those specific wounds and make you a better person because of it.

....

....

....

....

....

....

....

....

....

....

....

....

....

....

....

....

....

....

....

....

....

....

Can you identify areas where the way you think, feel, or behave does not reflect the truth? Ask God to open your eyes to those areas. As He exposes the lies, write the opposite of it—the truth—below. Praise Him for that revelation that He will be using to lead you to your restoration.

....
....
....
....
....
....
....
....
....
....
....
....
....
....
....
....
....
....

"When we put ourselves in God's healing hands, we may begin
broken and damaged, but we end up whole and complete,
without any evidence we were ever marred."

Chapter 12

THE WOUNDS OF SIN

*Y*ou can trust God with all the mistakes of your past. He is able to heal and save to the uttermost (Hebrews 7:25). No one is beyond His reach—not you, and not the people you may have hurt.

I acknowledged my sin to You, and my iniquity I did not hide.
I said, I will confess my transgressions to the Lord
[continually unfolding the past till all is told]—then You
[instantly] forgave me the guilt and iniquity of my sin.
Selah [pause, and calmly think of that]!

PSALM 32:5

*H*ow does the following quote connect to the theme of this chapter? How can it influence your personal journey of soul healing?

My wounds are loathsome and corrupt because of my foolishness. —PSALM 38:5

....

....

....

....

....

....

....

....

....

....

....

....

....

....

....

....

....

....

....

....

....

....

....

....

....

....

....

....

*I*f God knows everything we do at all times, why is it important for us to acknowledge our wrongdoing to Him? What kind of response can we expect from God?

*I*n Psalm 32:3–4, how does David describe how he felt during his time of unconfessed sin? Has there been a time in your life when you felt conviction, and ignored it? How did it feel? Pray and ask God for a heart sensitive to His conviction in your life, especially with your family relationships. Record what He reveals below.

....

....

....

....

....

....

....

....

....

....

....

....

....

....

....

....

....

....

....

"Talking about the things that are hidden in darkness
is often the very thing that releases us from them."

Surely He has borne our griefs (sicknesses, weaknesses, and distresses) and carried our sorrows and pains [of punishment], yet we [ignorantly] considered Him stricken, smitten, and afflicted by God [as if with leprosy]. But He was wounded for our transgressions, He was bruised for our guilt and iniquities; the chastisement [needful to obtain] peace and well-being for us was upon Him, and with the stripes [that wounded] Him we are healed and made whole. —ISAIAH 53:4–5

*W*hat does this Bible verse mean to you? According to this verse, why is it not acceptable to God for you to continue to punish yourself?

....

....

....

....

....

....

....

....

....

....

....

....

....

....

....

....

*F*or each offense you are punishing yourself for, write a prayer of thanks for Jesus being your substitute, and forgiving you. Confess the prayer as often as necessary.

....

....

....

....

....

....

....

....

....

....

....

....

....

....

....

....

....

....

"Jesus became our substitute—He has suffered and has been punished for our sins. He was wounded for our transgressions. His wounds have healed our wounds, but that only becomes a reality in our life when we believe it and let go of the past."

"We are invited into a relationship
of trusting God for absolutely everything,
and one of those things is trusting Him
to take care of the past with all of our mistakes
and the pain we experience from them."

Chapter 13

LEARNING TO LIVE INSIDE OUT

*W*hen we accept Christ as our Savior, He does an amazing work in us. He comes to live inside of us and gives us a new nature and a new spirit, both of which are His. Everything that Jesus is comes to live inside of us, in our born-again spirit.

His divine power has bestowed upon us all things
that [are requisite and suited] to life and godliness,
through the [full, personal] knowledge
of Him Who called us by and to His own
glory and excellence (virtue).

2 PETER 1:3

*H*ow does the following quote connect to the theme of this chapter? How can it influence your personal journey of soul healing?

> *I have been crucified with Christ. It is no longer I who live, but Christ who lives in me.*
> *And the life I now live in the flesh I live by faith in the Son of God,*
> *who loved me and gave himself for me.* —GALATIANS 2:20 ESV

....

....

....

....

....

....

....

....

....

....

....

....

....

....

....

....

....

....

....

....

....

....

*A*re you trusting God to change your true nature, or are you trying on your own to be a "good Christian"? Write a few trust statements for what you've tried unsuccessfully to change in your life. Pray them out loud in faith.

"God, You alone are powerful to.... I trust You to...."

....

....

....

....

....

....

....

....

....

....

....

....

....

....

....

....

....

....

....

....

*D*o you find it difficult to accept how God made you? Write a thank-you note to God, mentioning five of the unique qualities about you that you may not have appreciated in the past.

....

....

....

....

....

....

....

....

....

....

....

....

....

....

....

....

....

....

"Please read and study Psalm 139 slowly. Contemplate all it is saying and thank God for creating you. You are not a mistake; you are God's amazing design!"

However, I am telling you nothing but the truth when I say it is profitable (good, expedient, advantageous) for you that I go away. Because if I do not go away, the Comforter (Counselor, Helper, Advocate, Intercessor, Strengthener, Standby) will not come to you [into close fellowship with you]; but if I go away, I will send Him to you [to be in close fellowship with you]. —JOHN 16:7

*W*hat does this Bible verse mean to you? Do you believe that the Holy Spirit is in you and desires close fellowship with you? What habits would you establish that would help make that relationship more personal?

....

....

....

....

....

....

....

....

....

....

....

....

....

....

....

....

....

....

The following verses include some of the things that God says are ours in Christ. Choose three of the verses and write them here, inserting your name in place of "you" or "we."

Colossians 2:10	1 Peter 1:16
Ephesians 4:2–6	1 Corinthians 2:16
Romans 8:2	Philippians 2:5
Isaiah 54:14	Philippians 4:7
1 John 5:18	1 John 4:4
Ephesians 1:4	Romans 5:17

....

....

....

....

....

....

....

....

....

....

....

....

....

....

....

....

"We begin our walk with God by believing His promises are true, and only then will we begin to experience the reality of them in our daily lives."

Chapter 14

You've Got What It Takes

*Y*ou are stronger than you may think you are. You can do whatever you need to do in life *through Christ,* and God's Word says that you are more than a conqueror through Him, who loves you.... We need to be determined and refuse to give up, but the greatest amount of determination will eventually dissipate unless we continually draw on God's strength that is in us.

Yet amid all these things we are more
than conquerors and gain a surpassing victory
through Him Who loved us.

Romans 8:37

*H*ow does the following quote connect to the theme of this chapter? How can it influence your personal journey of soul healing?

> *I can do all things [which He has called me to do] through Him who strengthens and empowers me [to fulfill His purpose—I am self-sufficient in Christ's sufficiency; I am ready for anything and equal to anything through Him who infuses me with inner strength and confident peace].* —PHILIPPIANS 4:13 AMP

....

....

....

....

....

....

....

....

....

....

....

....

....

....

....

....

....

....

....

*W*hat does it mean to be *more* than a conqueror? Is that how you see yourself? Why or why not? Why is what we believe about ourselves important?

....

....

....

....

....

....

....

....

....

....

....

....

....

....

....

....

....

....

....

....

....

....

....

....

....

....

....

*A*re you dealing with anything right now in your life that feels overwhelming? Read Psalm 119:28 and Psalm 22:19, then write your own psalm, expressing your belief that God is your strength.

....

....

....

....

....

....

....

....

....

....

....

....

....

....

....

....

....

....

....

....

....

....

"Learning to believe and trust in God's Word more than we believe what we think or feel makes the difference in living victoriously or being defeated."

Those who hope in the LORD will renew their strength.
They will soar on wings like eagles; they will run and not grow weary,
they will walk and not be faint. —ISAIAH 40:31 NIV

*W*hat does this Bible verse mean to you? Describe an area in your life where you need renewed strength. Entrust it to God by writing a prayer using the language of Isaiah 40:31, inserting "I" and "my."

....

....

....

....

....

....

....

....

....

....

....

....

....

....

....

....

....

....

....

*H*ave you had any thoughts of hope that came out of nowhere when you were in the middle of a season of hopelessness? Explain.

....

....

....

....

....

....

....

....

....

....

....

....

....

....

....

....

....

....

....

....

"When I was a young girl of nine or ten, I recall lying in bed thinking, Someday I'm going to do something great!... *I realize now that those thoughts began to slip into my mind only after I received Christ as Savior at the age of nine."*

Chapter 15

ROADBLOCKS TO HEALING

*W*hen we are wounded, we must not only desire to be healed, but we must be willing and ready to be brutally honest with ourselves. The truth makes us free (John 8:32), but facing truth is not always easy. We develop many ways to hide from truth, and they become roadblocks and hindrances to our healing.

I acknowledged my sin to You, and my iniquity I did not hide.
I said, I will confess my transgressions to the Lord
[continually unfolding the past till all is told]—then You
[instantly] forgave me the guilt and iniquity of my sin.

PSALM 32:5

*H*ow does the following quote connect to the theme of this chapter? How can it influence your personal journey of soul healing?

> *It will be said: "Build up, build up, prepare the road!*
> *Remove the obstacles out of the way of my people."* —ISAIAH 57:14 NIV

....

....

....

....

....

....

....

....

....

....

....

....

....

....

....

....

....

....

....

*H*ow will following God instead of your feelings help you on your journey of healing? Why do you think finally facing the hurtful facts is healing?

....

....

....

....

....

....

....

....

....

....

....

....

....

....

....

....

....

....

....

....

....

....

....

*A*re you ready to let go of any hindrances that are keeping you from getting well? Let a loving Father God help you dig up your hurt so you can deal with it. Explain any circumstance you thought you could leave behind that ended up following you.

....
....
....
....
....
....
....
....
....
....
....
....
....
....
....
....
....
....
....
....
....

"Buried feelings have energies of their own. They are alive,
and they constantly affect us in adverse ways
until we confront and deal with them."

Although my father and my mother have forsaken me, yet the Lord will take me up [adopt me as His child]. —PSALM 27:10

*W*hat does this Bible verse mean to you? Are there any circumstances from the previous question that are a result of something either of your parents did or didn't do? Have you felt forsaken by anyone else? Explain.

....

....

....

....

....

....

....

....

....

....

....

....

....

....

....

....

....

....

....

....

....

*A*re there issues in your life that you are blaming others for or making excuses? Spend a few minutes with God, asking Him to help you recognize any areas where you need to take ownership, and write anything He reveals below. Follow it up with any needed apologies.

....

....

....

....

....

....

....

....

....

....

....

....

....

....

....

....

....

....

....

"We will find real freedom if we learn to simply say,
'I'm sorry and there is no excuse for my behavior.'"

"I often say there are two kinds of pain we can choose between: the pain of going forward or the pain of remaining where we are. Even though facing truth and going forward is painful, at least it is a type of pain that allows us to make progress, and that is far better than ongoing pain that will never end."

Chapter 16

THE ROADBLOCK OF SELF-PITY

*S*elf-pity won't go away on its own. We have to stop feeding it, and that means we need to stop giving in to it. I learned that just because my enemy, the devil, was inviting me to a pity party, it didn't mean I had to attend.

Praised (honored, blessed) be the God and Father of
our Lord Jesus Christ (the Messiah)! By His boundless mercy
we have been born again to an ever-living hope through
the resurrection of Jesus Christ from the dead.

1 PETER 1:3

$\mathcal{H}$ow does the following quote connect to the theme of this chapter? How can it influence your personal journey of soul healing?

As Christians we should never feel sorry for ourselves.
The moment we do so we lose our energy, we lose the will to fight
and the will to live and are paralyzed. —MARTYN LLOYD-JONES

....

....

....

....

....

....

....

....

....

....

....

....

....

....

....

....

....

....

....

Self-pity is a debilitating sin that paralyzes us from progress in our lives. Are there areas of stalled growth in your life? Can any of it be traced back to self-pity? Explain.

*F*our antidotes that can help with the sickness of self-pity are to be aggressively thankful, to do something for someone else, to just get up and go do something, and to find something that you can laugh about. In the lines below, write some ideas about what you could get up and do in the heat of self-pity.

....
....
....
....
....
....
....
....
....
....
....
....
....
....
....
....
....
....
....

*"Self-pity comes from an unwillingness to accept
a situation or circumstance in your life."*

Now the doings (practices) of the flesh are clear (obvious): they are immorality, impurity, indecency, idolatry, sorcery, enmity, strife, jealousy, anger (ill temper), selfishness, divisions (dissensions), party spirit (factions, sects with peculiar opinions, heresies), envy, drunkenness, carousing, and the like. I warn you beforehand, just as I did previously, that those who do such things shall not inherit the kingdom of God. —GALATIANS 5:19–21

*W*hat does this Bible verse mean to you? How is self-pity like idolatry?

....
....
....
....
....
....
....
....
....
....
....
....
....
....
....
....
....
....

*W*rite any triggers to self-pity in your life, then write something related that you can be thankful about instead.

Example:
Being the only one responsible for cleaning the house.
THANKFUL FOR: a husband who helps when I ask, who doesn't complain and criticize, a house that isn't big.

....

....

....

....

....

....

....

....

....

....

....

....

....

....

....

....

....

....

"Sometime during one of my pity parties, I heard God speak
in my spirit and say, 'You can be pitiful or powerful,
but you can't be both. Which one will you choose?'"

Chapter 17

STAND UP FOR YOURSELF

*Y*our painful past doesn't ever have to be your destiny—you can take a stand against the wrong behavior of other people who have harmed you, and when you do, you will feel empowered, rather than merely feeling like a helpless victim. People who are being abused or mistreated need to be courageous, speak up, and take a stand to protect themselves.

He gives power to the faint, and to him
who has no might he increases strength.

ISAIAH 40:29 ESV

*H*ow does the following quote connect to the theme of this chapter? How can it influence your personal journey of soul healing?

> *Courage is contagious. When a brave man takes a stand,*
> *the spines of others are often stiffened.* —BILLY GRAHAM

....

....

....

....

....

....

....

....

....

....

....

....

....

....

....

....

....

....

....

....

Is there someone in your life who is mistreating you whom you need to confront? Can you identify why you haven't? Pray that God would give you wisdom, courage, and grace, then practice by writing below what you need to say.

....

....

....

....

....

....

....

....

....

....

....

....

....

....

....

....

....

....

....

....

....

....

*H*ow is avoiding necessary confrontation a way to deny someone God's best for that person?

....

....

....

....

....

....

....

....

....

....

....

....

....

....

....

....

....

....

....

....

"Abusers usually disrespect people who
meekly put up with their bad behavior. A part of them
actually wants someone to confront them."

A gentle answer turns away wrath,
but a harsh word stirs up anger. —PROVERBS 15:1 NIV

*W*hat does this Bible verse mean to you? Besides word choice, what other things will communicate gentleness when we talk to someone? Once you have confronted with grace, does the other person's response determine whether or not you did the right thing?

....

....

....

....

....

....

....

....

....

....

....

....

....

....

....

....

....

....

....

*I*f you have been seriously mistreated, you may be inaccurately judging things and people through your pain. God's Word can guide you into what is right and balanced. Write a prayer of relinquishment, declaring your submission to God's Word as the supreme authority in your life. Record the inaccuracies He reveals and the verses He uses to contradiction your old way of life and lead you to victory.

....

....

....

....

....

....

....

....

....

....

....

....

....

....

....

....

....

"The only way I learned what right behavior
is came through studying God's Word."

Chapter 18

ESTABLISH BOUNDARIES— DON'T BUILD WALLS

*I*t is important for us to establish boundaries in all areas of our lives. Healthy boundaries are safety nets for us and other people, but we do need to be sure that we truly are setting boundaries, not building walls.... If you have built walls in your heart to keep others from hurting you, only you can tear them down. If you don't, you can never love or really receive love in return.

Rather, let our lives lovingly express truth [in all things, speaking truly, dealing truly, living truly]. Enfolded in love, let us grow up in every way and in all things into Him Who is the Head, [even] Christ (the Messiah, the Anointed One).

EPHESIANS 4:15

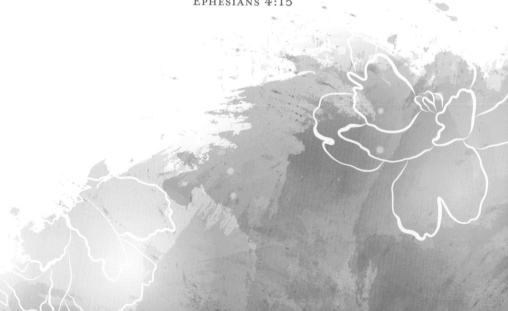

How does the following quote connect to the theme of this chapter? How can it influence your personal journey of soul healing?

You get what you tolerate. —HENRY CLOUD

....

....

....

....

....

....

....

....

....

....

....

....

....

....

....

....

....

....

....

....

....

*T*hink back on the times when you have been asked for a favor. What ran through your head before you gave an answer? Did you follow your emotions—wanting to please that person—or your heart, wanting to please God?

*W*as there a time you felt confronted by God (Revelation 3:19)? What impression did it leave on you of God's character?

....
....
....
....
....
....
....
....
....
....
....
....
....
....
....
....
....
....
....
....
....
....

*"Love reproves and chastises in addition to helping and giving.
We truly do not love another person if we let them
take advantage of us. God confronts us for our own good,
and He does it because He loves us."*

Receive instruction in wise dealing and *the discipline of wise thoughtfulness, righteousness, justice, and integrity.* —PROVERBS 1:3

*W*hat does this Bible verse mean to you? What do you think is the difference between what appears as thoughtfulness and *wise* thoughtfulness?

....

....

....

....

....

....

....

....

....

....

....

....

....

....

....

....

....

....

....

....

....

....

*A*re you aware of unhealthy responses inside you that happen automatically when your feelings are hurt or you perceive rejection? Is your response a result of a vow you made to yourself that needs to be broken? Pray that God would give you wisdom into your own behavior, then write what God reveals to you. Follow with a confession and request for God's power to restore you with healthy boundaries.

....
....
....
....
....
....
....
....
....
....
....
....
....
....
....
....
....

"When we have walls in our heart and refuse to let people in, those walls become hindrances that actually prevent us from growing spiritually in our relationship with God."

"When we stand up for ourselves
we are not trying to control
what other people do,
but rather we are controlling
what they do to us."

Chapter 19

BECOME YOUR OWN BEST ALLY

*I*t is time that we make a decision to agree with God rather than our enemies. Perhaps you have formed an opinion of yourself based on what unkind people have said or thought about you, or how they have treated you. If so, that is a mistake that needs to be corrected. It is time for you to be for you.

I am not conscious of anything against myself, and I feel blameless;
but I am not vindicated and acquitted before God on that account.
It is the Lord [Himself] Who examines and judges me.

1 CORINTHIANS 4:4

*H*ow does the following quote connect to the theme of this chapter? How can it influence your personal journey of soul healing?

> *Like the fairy tale suggests, the "mirror, mirror on the wall" shows us the face of our enemy.... We defeat ourselves far more than we are defeated by external circumstances.* —JOHN MAXWELL

....

....

....

....

....

....

....

....

....

....

....

....

....

....

....

....

....

....

....

*T*hink of yourself when you were a young girl. Write a message to her, apologizing for not standing up for her. Offer your friendship, your loyalty, your lifelong commitment to show kindness and acceptance and grace. Tell her the good and the gifts you see in her/yourself.

*H*ow often do you base your opinion of yourself on the opinion others have of you? Decide now to believe only what God says about you, and write that in a prayer to Him. Explain how humility and confidence can both be yours. How can humility free you to be who you are and enable you to do your best for God?

....

....

....

....

....

....

....

....

....

....

....

....

....

....

....

....

....

....

....

"The dread of criticism can be the death of greatness."

If any of you is deficient in wisdom, let him ask of the giving God [Who gives] to everyone liberally and ungrudgingly, without reproaching or faultfinding, and it will be given him. Only it must be in faith that he asks with no wavering (no hesitating, no doubting). For the one who wavers (hesitates, doubts) is like the billowing surge out at sea that is blown hither and thither and tossed by the wind. —JAMES 1:5–6

*W*hat does this Bible verse mean to you? Is fear making you indecisive? How does your self-doubt hinder your growth in God?

....

....

....

....

....

....

....

....

....

....

....

....

....

....

....

....

....

....

....

....

*I*t is important to believe that you can make good decisions. List each important decision you face, and praise God for His perfect love that casts away fear. Be sure to leave room to record praise for the result of your decisions.

....

....

....

....

....

....

....

....

....

....

....

....

....

....

....

....

....

....

....

....

....

"If you constantly do what people think you should do instead of following your own heart, you are denying who you are and the right God has given you to make choices of your own."

Chapter 20

HEALING THE WOUNDS
OF CODEPENDENCY

*I*t wounds our own souls to watch the people we love wound theirs. It is always good to try to help the people we care about who are hurting, but when helping them begins to destroy us, then we have to stop.... When a person is codependent, it means that their life is controlled by someone else's problems or bad choices.

Casting the whole of your care [all your anxieties,
all your worries, all your concerns, once and for all]
on Him, for He cares for you affectionately
and cares about you watchfully.

1 PETER 5:7

*H*ow does the following quote connect to the theme of this chapter? How can it influence your personal journey of soul healing?

I was your cure, and you were my disease. I was saving you, but you were killing me!
—AUTHOR UNKNOWN

....

....

....

....

....

....

....

....

....

....

....

....

....

....

....

....

....

....

....

....

....

*W*hat does it mean to help someone more by not helping them? Describe any relationship in your life where this might be true.

....

....

....

....

....

....

....

....

....

....

....

....

....

....

....

....

....

....

....

....

....

....

....

....

*P*art of God's restoration includes giving you discernment about when you should take a stand and when you should give in and do what someone asks. Write a prayer thanking God for His promised wisdom. Thank Him that His power to communicate with you is greater than any perceived inability to hear Him.

....

....

....

....

....

....

....

....

....

....

....

....

....

....

....

....

....

"It is not uncommon for troubled people to never be willing
to make a change as long as they have someone
who continues rescuing them."

Lean on, trust in, and *be confident in the Lord with all your heart* and *mind and do not rely on your own insight* or *understanding.* —PROVERBS 3:5

*W*hat does this Bible verse mean to you? What are some specific problem areas where you need to trust God for His understanding, rather than continuing with what you've always done in the past?

....

....

....

....

....

....

....

....

....

....

....

....

....

....

....

....

....

....

....

*I*f you are unsure whether you are helping or giving too much, take a few minutes to honestly examine your motives. Write what you are doing, then tell how the action makes you feel afterward. Has a short-term blessing turned into an ongoing, thankless obligation? Are your actions fostering dependence? Pray for God's wisdom on how to move forward.

....

....

....

....

....

....

....

....

....

....

....

....

....

....

....

....

....

....

"His grace is sufficient even in situations that are more painful than we could have ever imagined."

Chapter 21

THE BLESSINGS OF A HEALTHY SOUL

*L*ooking at the end from the beginning of a painful journey helps us not turn back when it is difficult. Since you may not have made your journey yet, you might not be aware of all the blessings that await you.... I hope to help you see what is waiting for you as you work with God toward having a healthy soul.

Looking away [from all that will distract] to Jesus,
Who is the Leader and the Source of our faith...and is also
its Finisher [bringing it to maturity and perfection].
He, for the joy [of obtaining the prize] that was set before Him,
endured the cross, despising and ignoring the shame,
and is now seated at the right hand of the throne of God.

HEBREWS 12:2

*H*ow does the following quote connect to the theme of this chapter? How can it influence your personal journey of soul healing?

> *Bless the LORD, O my soul; and all that is within me, bless His holy name!*
> *Bless the LORD, O my soul, and forget not all His benefits: Who forgives all your iniquities,*
> *Who heals all your diseases.* —PSALM 103:1–3 NKJV

....

....

....

....

....

....

....

....

....

....

....

....

....

....

....

....

....

....

....

....

....

....

....

....

*A*s you continue your journey of healing, there are many things to look forward to, including better health, increased energy, and more confidence. What are some dream projects or activities you would like to tackle once you have the health, energy, and confidence?

....

....

....

....

....

....

....

....

....

....

....

....

....

....

....

....

....

....

....

....

....

....

....

$\mathcal{D}$oing things in a new way requires diligence, but what may feel almost impossible to you right now will one day be easy if you don't give up. Write your own psalm of praise, using Psalm 103:2–5 as a template if you'd like. Insert your name or "my" in place of "your," and be specific with your sin, your diseases, your pit.

....

....

....

....

....

....

....

....

....

....

....

....

....

....

....

....

....

....

....

"God always rewards those who are diligent in seeking Him"

(Hebrews 11:6).

A happy heart is good medicine and
a cheerful mind works healing. —PROVERBS 17:22

What does this Bible verse mean to you? Write about someone whose demeanor and outlook has been like good medicine to you.

....

....

....

....

....

....

....

....

....

....

....

....

....

....

....

....

....

....

....

....

....

....

....

....

*A*s you anticipate your healing, it is wise to reach out and help others. God sometimes gives us the ability to help others, even when we can't seem to solve our own problems. List some ideas, big or small, of how you can do good and help specific people in your life.

....

....

....

....

....

....

....

....

....

....

....

....

....

....

....

....

....

....

"As we help others, we are sowing seed that brings back
a harvest of blessing in our own lives."

"The world may call you a victim,
but God calls you victorious.
The world calls you damaged goods,
but God calls you His daughter."

Chapter 22

THE PAINLESS PATH

*W*hen we truly want to hear from God, He will speak to us, but we may not always like what we hear. We usually want something that is easy to do, but God wants to give us grace (ease) to do very difficult things. Doing the right thing when everything about it feels wrong is the pathway to progress.

Enter through the narrow gate; for wide is the gate and spacious
and broad is the way that leads away to destruction,
and many are those who are entering through it.
But the gate is narrow (contracted by pressure) and the way
is straitened and compressed that leads away to life,
and few are those who find it.

MATTHEW 7:13–14

*H*ow does the following quote connect to the theme of this chapter? How can it influence your personal journey of soul healing?

What comes easy won't last, what lasts won't come easy. —AUTHOR UNKNOWN

....

....

....

....

....

....

....

....

....

....

....

....

....

....

....

....

....

....

....

....

*W*hen people talk about others who have bad tempers, are terribly insecure, want to control others, or are ruled by fear, they often say: "They have a lot of baggage!" Do you identify with anything in that list? Reflect and write any triggers (traffic? telemarketers? a child's bad decision?), then write a sincere prayer of relinquishment and your desire to leave the baggage behind.

*P*lease don't make the mistake of only looking at how far you still have to go. God is not impatient with any kind of progress. Ask Him for insight, then record any progress He reveals in your life.

....

....

....

....

....

....

....

....

....

....

....

....

....

....

....

....

....

....

....

....

"The Holy Spirit will lead you at a pace that is right for you,
and along the way you can appreciate and celebrate
each little victory that you have."

They will be like a tree planted by the water that sends out its roots by the stream. It does not fear when heat comes; its leaves are always green. It has no worries in a year of drought and never fails to bear fruit. —JEREMIAH 17:8 NIV

*W*hat does this Bible verse mean to you? What does the stream represent to you? How will you send out a root to it?

....
....
....
....
....
....
....
....
....
....
....
....
....
....
....
....
....
....
....
....
....

*W*hat things has God been leading you to do regularly as part of your healing journey? What new level of commitment with Him could He be asking from you in order to care for your wounds?

....

....

....

....

....

....

....

....

....

....

....

....

....

....

....

....

....

....

....

*"Our wounds heal by degrees. It takes time and persistence
in doing the right thing to properly care for the wound."*

Chapter 23

THE GREAT EXCHANGE

*J*esus invites us to live an exchanged life. On any day, we can exchange a bad attitude for a good one, our sins for forgiveness, our failures for mercy, hopelessness for hope, and thousands of other good things. But we don't get the new one until we turn in the old one.

For our sake He made Christ [virtually] to be sin Who knew no sin,
so that in and through Him we might become [endued with,
viewed as being in, and examples of] the righteousness of God
[what we ought to be, approved and acceptable
and in right relationship with Him, by His goodness].

2 CORINTHIANS 5:21

*H*ow does the following quote connect to the theme of this chapter? How can it influence your personal journey of soul healing?

The Spirit of the Sovereign LORD is on me, because the LORD has anointed me to proclaim good news to the poor. He has sent me to bind up the brokenhearted, to proclaim freedom for the captives and release from darkness for the prisoners...to bestow on them a crown of beauty instead of ashes, the oil of joy instead of mourning, and a garment of praise instead of a spirit of despair. —ISAIAH 61:1–3 NIV

*I*s there a point in your life when you stopped living and started just surviving? Explain. Write a prayer of praise to Jesus for His desire and power to exchange the ashes of your past for a crown of beauty.

....
....
....
....
....
....
....
....
....
....
....
....
....
....
....
....
....
....
....
....
....
....
....

*E*xchange happens when we believe in Jesus, believe that His promises are for us, and take the steps of faith that He directs us to take. Write what specific steps you feel He is directing you to take.

....

....

....

....

....

....

....

....

....

....

....

....

....

....

....

....

....

....

"Don't let the fear of taking a stand hold you back from
being all you can be and doing all that you can do.
You will never be fulfilled and satisfied if you don't
fulfill your destiny. You are far too valuable to passively
let anyone abuse or misuse you. It is time to take a stand!"

*All that the Father has is mine; therefore I said that he will take
what is mine and declare it to you.* —JOHN 16:15 ESV

*W*hat does this Bible verse mean to you? What does Jesus have that you would
like declared to you?

....

....

....

....

....

....

....

....

....

....

....

....

....

....

....

....

....

....

....

....

....

*I*t is time to stop thinking continually "What is wrong with me?" God, because of His goodness in Jesus, views us as being right. Agree with God on this one. Write five things about yourself that are right.

....

....

....

....

....

....

....

....

....

....

....

....

....

....

....

....

....

....

"He not only opens the prison doors,
according to Isaiah, but He opens our eyes."

"Never forget that you are precious and dearly loved,
and that not only has Jesus gone before us
into heaven to prepare a place for us
where we will live with Him for eternity,
He has also arranged for us to live
a fulfilling and abundant life
during our journey here on earth."

ABOUT THE AUTHOR

JOYCE MEYER is one of the world's leading practical Bible teachers. A *New York Times* bestselling author, Joyce's books have helped millions of people find hope and restoration through Jesus Christ. Joyce's programs, *Enjoying Everyday Life* and *Everyday Answers with Joyce Meyer*, air around the world on television, radio, and the Internet. Through Joyce Meyer Ministries, Joyce teaches internationally on a number of topics with a particular focus on how the Word of God applies to our everyday lives. Her candid communication style allows her to share openly and practically about her experiences so others can apply what she has learned to their lives.

Joyce has authored more than one hundred books, which have been translated into more than one hundred languages, and over 65 million of her books have been distributed worldwide. Bestsellers include *Power Thoughts; The Confident Woman; Look Great, Feel Great; Starting Your Day Right; Ending Your Day Right; Approval Addiction; How to Hear from God; Beauty for Ashes;* and *Battlefield of the Mind.*

Joyce's passion to help hurting people is foundational to the vision of Hand of Hope, the missions arm of Joyce Meyer Ministries. Hand of Hope provides worldwide humanitarian outreaches such as feeding programs, medical care, orphanages, disaster response, human trafficking intervention and rehabilitation, and much more—always sharing the love and gospel of Christ.